Tuck Me In, God

Christine Harder Tangvald
Illustrated by Shelley Dieterichs

CPH.
SAINT LOUIS

Dear God!
 Hi, it's me, (say your name).
What a busy day this has been.
 Wow!

Did you see everything that happened today?
I know You did, God,
Because **You are with me** all the time, aren't You …
All day … Every day! And I am glad, God,
 Very, very GLAD!

God, did You see all the **people** in my day?
Here are some of the people I saw today:

family

mail carrier

friends

teacher

neighbor

check-out
clerk

Grandpa and Grandma

doctor

baby

aunt, uncle and cousins

minister

And I also saw _____.

Thank You, God, for all the wonderful *people* in my day.

And, God, did You see all the **places** in my day?
Here are some of the places I went today:

church

school

car

tub

Grandma's
house

drive-through

zoo

walk

grocery
store

my friend's
house

playground

mall

soccer
game

bed

And I also went to _____.

Thank You, God, for all the *places* in my wonderful day!

And did You see all the **_things I did_** today, God?
Today I:

got dressed
by myself

went to
school

went to
my music
lesson

played
hide-and-seek

helped

worked

took a nap

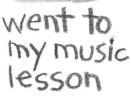
hugged
someone

played ball

went ice-skating

jumped rope

took a bath

went shopping

yum yum

ate a hamburger

rode my bike

watched TV

Not only that, but today I _____.

Wow! I was BUSY today, wasn't I?

Thank You, God, for all the wonderful *things to do* in my day!

All my days are special, God.
But sometimes I have a ***really special*** day!
Today was really special because:

I learned how to

_____.

I lost a tooth.

It was _____ 's
birthday.

It was Valentine's
Day.

We had a picnic.

It was
Thanksgiving.

It was
Christmas Day.

It was the Fourth
of July.

And today was *special* because _____.

Oh, yes. I *like* special days, God.

Thank You for **really special days!**

Did You hear me *laugh* today, God ... right out loud?

Today I laughed when _____.

Did You hear me **cry** today, God? _____.

I cried when _____

And sometimes I get *mad*.

Today I got mad when _____.

You care about how I **feel**, don't You, God?
Oh, yes. You want to know:

If I feel **glad**.

Or if I feel **sad**.

Or if I feel **mad**.

Or even if I feel very, very **BAD!**

You care about me because You *love* me, right?
I think I will talk to You about it *right now*!

Dear God, today I felt _____

because _____

_____

_____

_____.

Sometimes, God, I feel *sorry*.
Very,
very
SORRY!

Then I really need to talk to You, God.
You sent Jesus to pay for the bad things I do.
You will *forgive* me because of Jesus, won't You?
I need that.

Let's see, is there anything I feel
Sorry for today?

Yes, here it is: _____
_____
_____
_____.

There.
Now I feel better—lots better!
Whew!

There are other people I want to pray for, God.
Other people need Your help too.

Right now I want to pray for _____.

God, will You please_____

_____.

Thank You, God.

Sometimes *I* need Your help too, God.
Sometimes there are things I want to ask You for
   For myself.
Here is something I want to ask You for—for me!

God, will You please_____

_____

_____

_____?

Thank You, God.

Sometimes, God, I just need to talk to You
About something **important!**
I am so glad I can talk to You about *anything* I want to,
anytime I want to, from *anywhere* I want to!
And You always *hear* me, don't You, God?

Wow! That is *Great!*

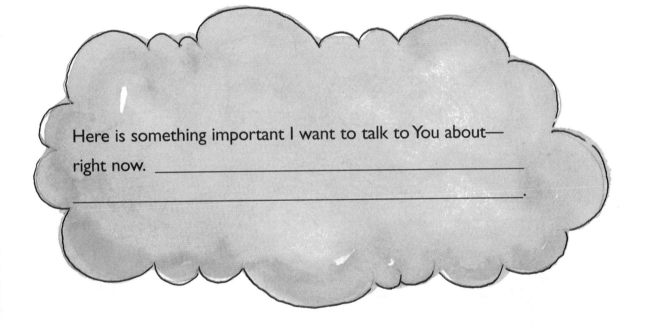

Here is something important I want to talk to You about—
right now. _____

_____.

Thank You for listening, God.
It feels so good when I talk to You about
Important Things!

God, You are **so good** to me!
I have so many things to tell You **thanks** for.

Yum-yum!   *Yum-yum!*   *Yum-yum!*

Thank You for **good food** to eat!

Today I ate _____

and _____

and _____.

Yum-yum!

Thank You, God, for my food.

Yum-yum!   *Yum-yum!*   *Yum-yum!*

Thank You, God, for Your *wonderful world*.
Today was:

sunny

rainy

cloudy

hot

cold

snowy

windy

And today I saw:

beautiful flowers

bright yellow leaves

birds flying

puffy white clouds

a wiggly worm

squirrels running

waves crashing

tall green trees

cows chewing

a red and pink sunset

Oh, yes. Thank You, God, for Your **wonderful world!**

my very Own

God, thank You for my *family*.
Thank You for my *friends*.
Thank You for my *home*.

Thank You for _____,

and_____,

and_____.

thank-You list

And *especially* thank You for sending Your Son,

Jesus,

to be my very own

friend and **Savior**.

Thank You, God, for

Everything!!!

I like to think about **tomorrow**, God.
Tomorrow is another day.
And every single day is brand-new.
I can choose some wonderful things to do.

Maybe I will do something *fun* like _____.

Maybe I will do something *important* like _____.

Maybe I will go _____.

And I might even _____.

Wow!
I think tomorrow will be a
VERY GOOD DAY!

And I will be talking to You, God,
because **You will be there with me**, won't You?
Oh, yes, You will! You are always right here with me.
That is the best part of tomorrow!

Hey!
Maybe I can tell someone **about You**, God!

Wouldn't **that** be great?
Maybe I can do **that** ...
TOMORROW!

God, You are
SO GREAT and **SO GOOD**.
It makes me want to say:

my very own Good-night Prayer!

_____

_____

_____

_____

Now,
Tuck me in, God—nice and *tight*!
Please, watch over me through this night.
Keep me safe and hear me pray—
Thank You, thank You, for this day.

Shhhh … Good night, God.   **Shhhh** … I'll sleep tight, God.

Shhhh … *Shhhhhh*…

Lights Out!